70 Sweet Ways to Help Kids Feel Special

by Susan Cutshall

Cincinnati, Ohio

Treatin' Kids Right: 70 Sweet Ways to Help Kids Feel Special
© 2000 Susan Cutshall

Standard Publishing, Cincinnati, Ohio
A division of Standex International Corporation
All rights reserved
Printed in the United States of America

07 06 05 04 03 02 01 00   5 4 3 2 1

ISBN: 0-7847-1238-7

Cover design by Jeff Jansen
Cover illustrations by Marc McBride
Interior design by Dale Meyers
Acquisition editor: Ruth Frederick
Project editor: Bruce E. Stoker

All Scripture quotations, unless otherwise indicated, are taken from the HOLY BIBLE, NEW INTERNATIONAL VERSION®. NIV®. Copyright © 1973, 1978, 1984 by International Bible Society. Used by permission of Zondervan Publishing House. All rights reserved.

Reproducible Pages
Permission is given to reproduce pages 11-80 for ministry purposes only—not for resale.

Introduction

In Matthew 18:10, Jesus said, "See that you do not look down on one of these little ones," and in Mark 10:14, "Let the little children come to me, and do not hinder them, for the kingdom of God belongs to such as these." How do you see the children in your church? Are they recognized as an important part of your congregation? Are you currently involved in evangelizing the children in your church's neighborhood or in your own neighborhood?

The purpose of this book is to help you reach any child in your life by giving him a special treat. It's easy! Choose an idea, copy it onto colored paper and attach the appropriate treat to the paper using snack-size, self-sealing plastic bags. (To help keep costs down, I generally use the snack-size candy bars and try to stock up during sales, especially after Halloween, Christmas, and Easter.) Next comes the fun part! Give it away! You are sure to receive a smile in return!

Need some ideas?
- Give them to children in your Sunday school class or as prizes during Children's church.
- Use them as rewards for Scripture memorization.
- Use them as an outreach tool simply by printing information about your church on the back of the paper.
- Have the kids in your class prepare the treats and then go out into your church's neighborhood (on Sunday morning!) and pass out the treats to all the children they see, personally inviting them to your church or a special event!
- Pass them out from your door as Halloween treats.
- Give them to children in your neighborhood to invite them to church.
- Use them in Christian schools as rewards and encouragers.
- Let your students think of creative ways to use them!

However you choose to use them, have fun spreading a little bit of fun and encouragement to God's precious children!

Celebrating children,

Susan

Scriptural Basis

We are all familiar with stories in the Bible that deal with children. Can you picture Miriam on the riverbank watching her baby brother Moses as he floated in a basket on the Nile? What about the Israelite slave girl in 2 Kings 5 who told Naaman's wife about the prophet Elisha who could heal the army commander's leprosy? Can you hear the happy sounds of the children shouting "Hosanna to the Son of David" in the temple courts as Jesus healed the blind and lame in Matthew 21:12-17? Can you feel the satisfaction of more than five thousand people who were fed by Jesus from a boy's lunch of bread and fish?

Certainly, children have played significant roles in God's plan for his people. Let's not forget the children all around us, for as important as they are to us, they are immensely more important to God. Let's not forget that children continue to work in God's plans, and so, let's not forget to encourage them as they grow, as they seek God's will, and as they minister to others.

Here are some verses that have helped me to see how important encouragement really is, especially when ministering with children.

"Therefore encourage one another and build each other up, just as in fact you are doing" (1 Thessalonians 5:11).

"But encourage one another daily, as long as it is called Today" (Hebrews 3:13).

"Let us not give up meeting together, as some are in the habit of doing, but let us encourage one another—and all the more as you see the Day approaching" (Hebrews 10:25).

Contents Checklist

Although there are no page numbers on the reproducible pages throughout the rest of the book, use this "table of contents" as a checklist to help you keep track of when you use each idea. Simply write the date when you use each idea in the space provided, and you will know when you last used each idea as you scan through the list. As an additional help, you may want to write the dates on a self-stick note and stick it on the appropriate page.

Section 1—General Ideas

- **Kids like you were "mint" to know Jesus!** (any mint)
Dates Used: _____

- **You are important to Jesus! That's no laughing matter!** (Snickers candy bar, a trademark of Mars, Inc.)
Dates Used: _____

- **Stick with Jesus every day!** (ReeseSticks wafer bar, a trademark of Hershey Foods Corp.)
Dates Used: _____

- **You were "maid" in the image of God!** (Brach's Milk Maid caramels, a trademark of Brach & Brock Confections, Inc.)
Dates Used: _____

- **Let God's great love for you bubble up and overflow!** (any bubble gum)
Dates Used: _____

- **God loves you from the top of your head to the tip of your toes!** (Warheads candy, a trademark of The Foreign Candy Company, Inc.)
Dates Used: _____

- **You can always count on Jesus to be your friend!** (foil-covered chocolate coins)
Dates Used: _____

- **God gave you something more precious than gold—his son, Jesus!** (Hershey's Nuggets with almonds—for the gold foil—a trademark of Hershey Foods Corp.)
Dates Used: _____

- **Whatever sport you play, be sure that you're on God's team!** (Nabisco's Sportz crackers, a trademark of Nabisco, Inc.)
Dates Used: _____

- **God is just waiting to pour his love on you!** (Betty Crocker's Gushers fruit snacks, a trademark of General Mills, Inc.)
Dates Used: _____

- **Did you know that God thinks you are "some-bunny" special?** (chocolate bunny—for Easter)
Dates Used: _____

- **You are "egg-stra" special to Jesus!** (chocolate egg—for Easter)
Dates Used: _____

- **Jesus died on the cross to save a world gummed up by sin!** (bubble gum—for Easter)
Dates Used: _____

- **No bones about it! God loves you!** (Brach's Dem Bones candies, a trademark of Brach & Brock Confections, Inc.—for Halloween)
Dates Used: _____

- **Don't blow a chance to thank God for all he's done for you!** (Charm's Blow Pop lollipop, a trademark of Charms L.P.—for Thanksgiving)
Dates Used: _____

- **You are "tree-mendously" important to Jesus!** (Reese's peanut butter tree, a trademark of Hershey Foods Corp.—for Christmas)
Dates Used: _____

- **God sent you the "purr-fect" gift—Jesus!** (Hershey's Kit Kat wafer bar, a trademark of Hershey Foods Corp.—for Christmas)
Dates Used: _____

Section 2–Teacher to Student

- **Hey, slugger! Step up to the plate and hit a homerun for Jesus!** (Nestle's Baby Ruth candy bar, a trademark of Nestle USA, Inc.)
Dates Used: _____

- **"Orange" you glad you're learning about Jesus?** (orange slices)
Dates Used: _____

- **It is such a joy to teach you about Jesus!** (Hershey's Almond Joy candy bar, a trademark of Hershey Foods Corp.)
Dates Used: _____

- **The Bible will always point you in the right direction!** (Nestle's Butterfinger candy bar, a trademark of Nestle USA, Inc.)
Dates Used: _____

- **Isn't it "amazin'" to learn how much God loves you?** (Amazin' Fruit gummy bears, a trademark of Hershey Foods Corp.)
Dates Used: _____

- **It is "beary" good to have you with us today!** (Nabisco's Teddy Grahams graham crackers, a trademark of Nabisco, Inc.)
Dates Used: _____

- **Why are we glad you're in this class? It would take all day to count the "Riesens"!** (Riesens candies, a trademark of Storck USA L.P.)
Dates Used: _____

- **We're glad you "popped" in today to learn about God's Word!** (popcorn)
Dates Used: _____

- **You are an important "piece" of this class!** (Reese's Pieces candies, a trademark of Hershey Foods Corp.)
Dates Used: _____

- **God loves us all! In his eyes there are no duds!** (Hershey's Milk Duds chocolate covered caramels, a trademark of Hershey Foods Corp.)
Dates Used: _____

- **It's so easy to get hooked on Jesus!** (Goldfish crackers, a trademark of Pepperidge Farms, Inc.)
Dates Used: _____

- **Study your Bible and be a "Word nerd" for Jesus!** (Willy Wonka Nerds, a trademark of Nestle USA, Inc.)
Dates Used: _____

- **You can learn s'more about God every day!** (a graham cracker, a marshmallow, and a piece of chocolate to make s'mores)
Dates Used: _____

- **Treasure God's Word and read the Bible every day!** (Brach's Special Treasures candies, a trademark of Brach & Brock Confections, Inc.)
Dates Used: _____

- **I have "bean" praying for you!** (jelly beans)
Dates Used: _____

- **Fill your head with the Word of God!** (Air Heads candies, a trademark of Van Melle, Inc.)
Dates Used: _____

- **You'll find mounds of help in God's Word!** (Mounds candy bar, a trademark of Hershey Foods Corp.)
Dates Used: _____

- **You help to make our class' "mix" more interesting!** (Chex snack mix, a trademark of General Mills, Inc.)
Dates Used: _____

- **There are plenty of good reasons for you to study the Bible!** (Good & Plenty candies, a trademark of Hershey Foods Corp.)
Dates Used: _____

- **Read and obey God's Word, and you'll be a smartie!** (Smarties candies, a trademark of CE DE Candy, Inc.)
Dates Used: _____

- **Any way you measure it, God's Word is awesome!** (Fruit by the Foot fruit snacks, a trademark of General Mills, Inc.)
Dates Used: _____

- **Don't be afraid to "ring" out the Good News about Jesus!** (ring-shaped candy or lollipops)
Dates Used: _____

- **Reading God's Word each day will help keep you on the right path!** (trail mix)
Dates Used: _____

- **It is a real treat to have you in this class!** (Kellogg's Rice Krispie Treats snacks, a trademark of Kellogg Company)
Dates Used: _____

- **Fill up your cup with the love of Jesus!** (Reese's peanut butter cups, a trademark of Hershey Foods Corp.)
Dates Used: _____

- **Jesus is the "Riesen" we can live today and eternally!** (Riesens candies, a trademark of Storck USA L.P.)
Dates Used: _____

- **We savor each chance we have to share God's love with you!** (Life Savers candies, a trademark of Lifesavers Company, Nabisco, Inc.)
Dates Used: _____

- **P B & J are so important! Prayer, the Bible, and Jesus!** (Russell Stover peanut butter and jelly cups, a trademark of Russell Stover Candies, Inc.)
Dates Used: _____

- **It is magnificent and marvelous fun having you in our class!** (M&M's chocolate candies, a trademark of Mars, Inc.)
Dates Used: _____

- **We have a whopping good time learning about Jesus!** (Hershey's Whoppers malted milk balls, a trademark of Hershey Foods Corp.)
Dates Used: _____

- **There are so "mini" wonderful things to learn in the Bible!** (Hershey's Miniatures chocolate bars, a trademark of Hershey Foods Corp.)
Dates Used: _____

Section 3-Scripture Reference

- **Don't forget! God keeps all his promises! Psalms 145:13** (Dove Promises chocolates, a trademark of Mars, Inc.)
Dates Used: _____

- **Every child is a superstar to Jesus! Mark 10:14** (Starburst fruit chews, a trademark of Mars, Inc.)
Dates Used: _____

- **Let's get to the heart of the matter—God loves you! John 3:16** (candy hearts—for Valentine's Day)
Dates Used: _____

- **The only wafer you to get to heaven is through Jesus Christ. John 14:6** (Nilla Wafers cookies, a trademark of Nabisco, Inc.)
Dates Used: _____

- **Love bears all things. 1 Corinthians 13:7** (gummy bears)
Dates Used: _____

- **You don't have to pay 100 grand for your salvation! It's a gift from God! Ephesians 2:8** (Nestle's 100 Grand candy bar, a trademark of Nestle USA, Inc.)
Dates Used: _____

- **God saved Noah, his family, and the animals, and he can save you! Hebrews 11:7** (animal crackers)
Dates Used: _____

Section 4-Scripture Verses

- "I have hidden your word in my heart that I might not sin against you." **Psalm 119:11** (chocolate candy heart)
Dates Used: _____

- Here's the scoop! "The Lord is gracious and compassionate, slow to anger and rich in love." **Psalm 145:8** (Fritos Scoops! corn chips, a trademark of Frito-Lay, Inc.)
Dates Used: _____

- "The Lord gives wisdom, and from his mouth come knowledge and understanding." **Proverbs 2:6** (Smarties candies, a trademark of CE DE Candy, Inc.)
Dates Used: _____

- "An honest answer is like a kiss on the lips." **Proverbs 24:26** (Hershey's Kisses chocolates, a trademark of Hershey Foods Corp.)
Dates Used: _____

- "Blessed are the pure in heart, for they will see God." **Matthew 5:8** (miniature marshmallows)
Dates Used: _____

- "Rejoice and be glad, because great is your reward in heaven." **Matthew 5:12** (Payday peanut caramel bar, a trademark of Hershey Foods Corp.)
Dates Used: _____

- Jesus said, "You are the salt of the earth!" **Matthew 5:13** (salted pretzels)
Dates Used: _____

- It is written, "How beautiful are the feet of those who bring good news!" **Romans 10:15** (Tootsie Roll chocolate chews, a trademark of Tootsie Roll Industries)
Dates Used: _____

- "Do not be overcome by evil, but overcome evil with good." **Romans 12:21** (Warheads candy, a trademark of The Foreign Candy Company, Inc.)
Dates Used: _____

- "God loves a cheerful giver." **2 Corinthians 9:7** (gold-foil-covered chocolate coins)
Dates Used: _____

- "The fruit of the Spirit is love, joy, peace, patience, kindness, goodness, faithfulness, gentleness, and self-control." **Galatians 5:22** (fruit snacks)
Dates Used: _____

- "Rejoice in the Lord always. I will say it again: Rejoice!" **Philippians 4:4** (Almond Joy candy bar, a trademark of Hershey Foods Corp.)
Dates Used: _____

- "Don't let anyone look down on you because you are young." **1 Timothy 4:12** (Nestle Baby Ruth, a trademark of Nestle USA, Inc.)
Dates Used: _____

- "Be ready to do whatever is good." **Titus 3:1** (Good & Plenty candy, a trademark of Hershey Foods Corp.)
Dates Used: _____

- "Jesus Christ is the same yesterday and today and forever." **Hebrews 13:8** (Now and Later candy, a trademark of Lifesaver Company, Nabisco, Inc.)
Dates Used: _____

Kids like you were **MINT** to know Jesus!

Kids like you were **MINT** to know Jesus!

Kids like you were **MINT** to know Jesus!

Kids like you were **MINT** to know Jesus!

You are important to Jesus! That's no **laughing** matter!

You are important to Jesus! That's no **laughing** matter!

You are important to Jesus! That's no **laughing** matter!

You are important to Jesus! That's no **laughing** matter!

Stick
with Jesus
every day!

Stick
with Jesus
every day!

Stick
with Jesus
every day!

Stick
with Jesus
every day!

You were "Maid" in the image of God!

You were "Maid" in the image of God!

You were "Maid" in the image of God!

You were "Maid" in the image of God!

Let God's great love for you **bubble up** and overflow!

Let God's great love for you **bubble up** and overflow!

Let God's great love for you **bubble up** and overflow!

Let God's great love for you **bubble up** and overflow!

God loves you from the top of your **HEAD** to the tip of your **TOES!**

God loves you from the top of your **HEAD** to the tip of your **TOES!**

God loves you from the top of your **HEAD** to the tip of your **TOES!**

God loves you from the top of your **HEAD** to the tip of your **TOES!**

You can always **COUNT** on Jesus to be your friend!

You can always **COUNT** on Jesus to be your friend!

You can always **COUNT** on Jesus to be your friend!

You can always **COUNT** on Jesus to be your friend!

GOD GAVE YOU SOMETHING MORE PRECIOUS THAN GOLD—
HIS SON, JESUS!

GOD GAVE YOU SOMETHING MORE PRECIOUS THAN GOLD—
HIS SON, JESUS!

GOD GAVE YOU SOMETHING MORE PRECIOUS THAN GOLD—
HIS SON, JESUS!

GOD GAVE YOU SOMETHING MORE PRECIOUS THAN GOLD—
HIS SON, JESUS!

WHATEVER SPORT YOU PLAY, BE SURE THAT **YOU'RE ON GOD'S TEAM!**

WHATEVER SPORT YOU PLAY, BE SURE THAT **YOU'RE ON GOD'S TEAM!**

WHATEVER SPORT YOU PLAY, BE SURE THAT **YOU'RE ON GOD'S TEAM!**

WHATEVER SPORT YOU PLAY, BE SURE THAT **YOU'RE ON GOD'S TEAM!**

GOD IS JUST WAITING TO **POUR** HIS LOVE ON YOU!

GOD IS JUST WAITING TO **POUR** HIS LOVE ON YOU!

GOD IS JUST WAITING TO **POUR** HIS LOVE ON YOU!

GOD IS JUST WAITING TO **POUR** HIS LOVE ON YOU!

Did you know that God thinks you are some-bunny special?

Did you know that God thinks you are some-bunny special?

Did you know that God thinks you are some-bunny special?

Did you know that God thinks you are some-bunny special?

You are **Egg-stra** special to Jesus!

You are **Egg-stra** special to Jesus!

You are **Egg-stra** special to Jesus!

You are **Egg-stra** special to Jesus!

Jesus died
on the cross
to save a world
**gummed
up**
by sin!

Jesus died
on the cross
to save a world
**gummed
up**
by sin!

Jesus died
on the cross
to save a world
**gummed
up**
by sin!

Jesus died
on the cross
to save a world
**gummed
up**
by sin!

No "Bones" about it!
God loves you!

No "Bones" about it!
God loves you!

No "Bones" about it!
God loves you!

No "Bones" about it!
God loves you!

Don't blow a chance
to thank God
for all he's done
for you!

Don't blow a chance
to thank God
for all he's done
for you!

Don't blow a chance
to thank God
for all he's done
for you!

Don't blow a chance
to thank God
for all he's done
for you!

You are
Tree-mendously
important to
Jesus!

You are
Tree-mendously
important to
Jesus!

You are
Tree-mendously
important to
Jesus!

You are
Tree-mendously
important to
Jesus!

God sent you the purr-fect gift —JESUS!

God sent you the purr-fect gift —JESUS!

God sent you the purr-fect gift —JESUS!

God sent you the purr-fect gift —JESUS!

HEY, SLUGGER!
*Step up to
the plate and*
HIT A HOMERUN
for Jesus!

HEY, SLUGGER!
*Step up to
the plate and*
HIT A HOMERUN
for Jesus!

HEY, SLUGGER!
*Step up to
the plate and*
HIT A HOMERUN
for Jesus!

HEY, SLUGGER!
*Step up to
the plate and*
HIT A HOMERUN
for Jesus!

"Orange" *you glad you're learning about* **Jesus?**

"Orange" *you glad you're learning about* **Jesus?**

"Orange" *you glad you're learning about* **Jesus?**

"Orange" *you glad you're learning about* **Jesus?**

It is such a
JOY
to teach you about Jesus!

It is such a
JOY
to teach you about Jesus!

It is such a
JOY
to teach you about Jesus!

It is such a
JOY
to teach you about Jesus!

The Bible will always **POINT** you in the right direction!

The Bible will always **POINT** you in the right direction!

The Bible will always **POINT** you in the right direction!

The Bible will always **POINT** you in the right direction!

Isn't it **AMAZIN'** to learn how much God loves you?

Isn't it **AMAZIN'** to learn how much God loves you?

Isn't it **AMAZIN'** to learn how much God loves you?

Isn't it **AMAZIN'** to learn how much God loves you?

IT IS BEARY GOOD TO HAVE YOU WITH US TODAY!

IT IS BEARY GOOD TO HAVE YOU WITH US TODAY!

IT IS BEARY GOOD TO HAVE YOU WITH US TODAY!

IT IS BEARY GOOD TO HAVE YOU WITH US TODAY!

Why are we glad
you're in this class?
It would take all day
to count the "Riesens"!

Why are we glad
you're in this class?
It would take all day
to count the "Riesens"!

Why are we glad
you're in this class?
It would take all day
to count the "Riesens"!

Why are we glad
you're in this class?
It would take all day
to count the "Riesens"!

We're glad you **POPPED** in today to learn about God's Word!

We're glad you **POPPED** in today to learn about God's Word!

We're glad you **POPPED** in today to learn about God's Word!

We're glad you **POPPED** in today to learn about God's Word!

You are an important "*Piece*" of this class!

You are an important "*Piece*" of this class!

You are an important "*Piece*" of this class!

You are an important "*Piece*" of this class!

God loves us all! In his eyes there are no DUDS!

God loves us all! In his eyes there are no DUDS!

God loves us all! In his eyes there are no DUDS!

God loves us all! In his eyes there are no DUDS!

It's so easy to get **HOOKED** on Jesus!

It's so easy to get **HOOKED** on Jesus!

It's so easy to get **HOOKED** on Jesus!

It's so easy to get **HOOKED** on Jesus!

STUDY YOUR BIBLE AND BE A **"WORD NERD"** FOR JESUS!

STUDY YOUR BIBLE AND BE A **"WORD NERD"** FOR JESUS!

STUDY YOUR BIBLE AND BE A **"WORD NERD"** FOR JESUS!

STUDY YOUR BIBLE AND BE A **"WORD NERD"** FOR JESUS!

You can learn **S'more** about God every day!

You can learn **S'more** about God every day!

You can learn **S'more** about God every day!

You can learn **S'more** about God every day!

Treasure
God's Word and read the Bible every day!

Treasure
God's Word and read the Bible every day!

Treasure
God's Word and read the Bible every day!

Treasure
God's Word and read the Bible every day!

I have "BEAN" praying for you!

I have "BEAN" praying for you!

I have "BEAN" praying for you!

I have "BEAN" praying for you!

FILL YOUR HEAD WITH THE WORD OF GOD!

FILL YOUR HEAD WITH THE WORD OF GOD!

FILL YOUR HEAD WITH THE WORD OF GOD!

FILL YOUR HEAD WITH THE WORD OF GOD!

You'll find **MOUNDS** of help in God's Word!

You'll find **MOUNDS** of help in God's Word!

You'll find **MOUNDS** of help in God's Word!

You'll find **MOUNDS** of help in God's Word!

There are **PLENTY** of **GOOD** reasons for you to study the Bible!

There are **PLENTY** of **GOOD** reasons for you to study the Bible!

There are **PLENTY** of **GOOD** reasons for you to study the Bible!

There are **PLENTY** of **GOOD** reasons for you to study the Bible!

Read and obey God's Word, and you'll be a *Smartie!*

Read and obey God's Word, and you'll be a *Smartie!*

Read and obey God's Word, and you'll be a *Smartie!*

Read and obey God's Word, and you'll be a *Smartie!*

Any way you measure it, God's Word is awesome!

Any way you measure it, God's Word is awesome!

Any way you measure it, God's Word is awesome!

Any way you measure it, God's Word is awesome!

Don't be afraid to
Ring Out
the Good News
about Jesus!

Don't be afraid to
Ring Out
the Good News
about Jesus!

Don't be afraid to
Ring Out
the Good News
about Jesus!

Don't be afraid to
Ring Out
the Good News
about Jesus!

Reading God's Word each day
will help keep you on the right path!

Reading God's Word each day
will help keep you on the right path!

Reading God's Word each day
will help keep you on the right path!

Reading God's Word each day
will help keep you on the right path!

It is a real
Treat
to have you
in this class!

It is a real
Treat
to have you
in this class!

It is a real
Treat
to have you
in this class!

It is a real
Treat
to have you
in this class!

Fill up your CUP with the love of Jesus!

Fill up your CUP with the love of Jesus!

Fill up your CUP with the love of Jesus!

Fill up your CUP with the love of Jesus!

Jesus is the "Riesen"
we can live today
and eternally!

Jesus is the "Riesen"
we can live today
and eternally!

Jesus is the "Riesen"
we can live today
and eternally!

Jesus is the "Riesen"
we can live today
and eternally!

We **savor** each chance we have to share God's love with you!

We **savor** each chance we have to share God's love with you!

We **savor** each chance we have to share God's love with you!

We **savor** each chance we have to share God's love with you!

PB & J

ARE SO IMPORTANT!

Prayer, the Bible, and Jesus!

PB & J

ARE SO IMPORTANT!

Prayer, the Bible, and Jesus!

PB & J

ARE SO IMPORTANT!

Prayer, the Bible, and Jesus!

PB & J

ARE SO IMPORTANT!

Prayer, the Bible, and Jesus!

It is
Magnificent
&
Marvelous
fun having you in our class!

We have a **WHOPPING** *good time learning about Jesus!*

We have a **WHOPPING** *good time learning about Jesus!*

We have a **WHOPPING** *good time learning about Jesus!*

We have a **WHOPPING** *good time learning about Jesus!*

There are so "mini" wonderful things to learn in the Bible!

There are so "mini" wonderful things to learn in the Bible!

There are so "mini" wonderful things to learn in the Bible!

There are so "mini" wonderful things to learn in the Bible!

**Don't forget!
God keeps
all his
*Promises!***

Psalms 145:13

**Don't forget!
God keeps
all his
*Promises!***

Psalms 145:13

**Don't forget!
God keeps
all his
*Promises!***

Psalms 145:13

**Don't forget!
God keeps
all his
*Promises!***

Psalms 145:13

Every child is a **SUPERSTAR** to Jesus!

Mark 10:14

Every child is a **SUPERSTAR** to Jesus!

Mark 10:14

Every child is a **SUPERSTAR** to Jesus!

Mark 10:14

Every child is a **SUPERSTAR** to Jesus!

Mark 10:14

Let's get to the **heart** of the matter
—God loves you!
John 3:16

Let's get to the **heart** of the matter
—God loves you!
John 3:16

Let's get to the **heart** of the matter
—God loves you!
John 3:16

Let's get to the **heart** of the matter
—God loves you!
John 3:16

The only "wafer" you to get to heaven is through Jesus Christ.
John 14:6

The only "wafer" you to get to heaven is through Jesus Christ.
John 14:6

The only "wafer" you to get to heaven is through Jesus Christ.
John 14:6

The only "wafer" you to get to heaven is through Jesus Christ.
John 14:6

Love BEARS all things.

1 Corinthians 13:7

Love BEARS all things.

1 Corinthians 13:7

Love BEARS all things.

1 Corinthians 13:7

Love BEARS all things.

1 Corinthians 13:7

You don't have to pay
100 Grand
for your salvation!
It's a gift from God!
Ephesians 2:8

God saved Noah,
his family, and the
ANIMALS,
and he can save YOU!
Hebrews 11:7

God saved Noah,
his family, and the
ANIMALS,
and he can save YOU!
Hebrews 11:7

God saved Noah,
his family, and the
ANIMALS,
and he can save YOU!
Hebrews 11:7

God saved Noah,
his family, and the
ANIMALS,
and he can save YOU!
Hebrews 11:7

"I have hidden your word in my heart that I might not sin against you."

Psalm 119:11

"I have hidden your word in my heart that I might not sin against you."

Psalm 119:11

"I have hidden your word in my heart that I might not sin against you."

Psalm 119:11

"I have hidden your word in my heart that I might not sin against you."

Psalm 119:11

Here's the scoop!
"The Lord is gracious
and compassionate,
slow to anger
and rich in love."

Psalm 145:8

Here's the scoop!
"The Lord is gracious
and compassionate,
slow to anger
and rich in love."

Psalm 145:8

Here's the scoop!
"The Lord is gracious
and compassionate,
slow to anger
and rich in love."

Psalm 145:8

Here's the scoop!
"The Lord is gracious
and compassionate,
slow to anger
and rich in love."

Psalm 145:8

"The Lord gives **Wisdom,** and from his mouth come **Knowledge** and **Understanding."**

Proverbs 2:6

"The Lord gives **Wisdom,** and from his mouth come **Knowledge** and **Understanding."**

Proverbs 2:6

"The Lord gives **Wisdom,** and from his mouth come **Knowledge** and **Understanding."**

Proverbs 2:6

"The Lord gives **Wisdom,** and from his mouth come **Knowledge** and **Understanding."**

Proverbs 2:6

"AN HONEST ANSWER IS LIKE A **Kiss** ON THE LIPS."

Proverbs 24:26

"AN HONEST ANSWER IS LIKE A **Kiss** ON THE LIPS."

Proverbs 24:26

"AN HONEST ANSWER IS LIKE A **Kiss** ON THE LIPS."

Proverbs 24:26

"AN HONEST ANSWER IS LIKE A **Kiss** ON THE LIPS."

Proverbs 24:26

"Blessed are the pure in heart, for they will see God."

Matthew 5:8

"Blessed are the pure in heart, for they will see God."

Matthew 5:8

"Blessed are the pure in heart, for they will see God."

Matthew 5:8

"Blessed are the pure in heart, for they will see God."

Matthew 5:8

"Rejoice and be glad, because **GREAT** is your reward in heaven."
Matthew 5:12

"Rejoice and be glad, because **GREAT** is your reward in heaven."
Matthew 5:12

"Rejoice and be glad, because **GREAT** is your reward in heaven."
Matthew 5:12

"Rejoice and be glad, because **GREAT** is your reward in heaven."
Matthew 5:12

Jesus said, "You are the SALT of the earth!"
Matthew 5:13

Jesus said, "You are the SALT of the earth!"
Matthew 5:13

Jesus said, "You are the SALT of the earth!"
Matthew 5:13

Jesus said, "You are the SALT of the earth!"
Matthew 5:13

IT IS WRITTEN, "How beautiful are the feet of those who bring good news!"
ROMANS 10:15

IT IS WRITTEN, "How beautiful are the feet of those who bring good news!"
ROMANS 10:15

IT IS WRITTEN, "How beautiful are the feet of those who bring good news!"
ROMANS 10:15

IT IS WRITTEN, "How beautiful are the feet of those who bring good news!"
ROMANS 10:15

"Do not be overcome by evil, but overcome evil with good."

Romans 12:21

"Do not be overcome by evil, but overcome evil with good."

Romans 12:21

"Do not be overcome by evil, but overcome evil with good."

Romans 12:21

"Do not be overcome by evil, but overcome evil with good."

Romans 12:21

"God loves a cheerful giver."
2 Corinthians 9:7

"God loves a cheerful giver."
2 Corinthians 9:7

"God loves a cheerful giver."
2 Corinthians 9:7

"God loves a cheerful giver."
2 Corinthians 9:7

"The fruit of the Spirit is love, joy, peace, patience, kindness, goodness, faithfulness, gentleness, and self-control."

Galatians 5:22

"The fruit of the Spirit is love, joy, peace, patience, kindness, goodness, faithfulness, gentleness, and self-control."

Galatians 5:22

"The fruit of the Spirit is love, joy, peace, patience, kindness, goodness, faithfulness, gentleness, and self-control."

Galatians 5:22

"The fruit of the Spirit is love, joy, peace, patience, kindness, goodness, faithfulness, gentleness, and self-control."

Galatians 5:22

"Rejoice in the Lord always. I will say it again: **Rejoice!**"

Philippians 4:4

"Rejoice in the Lord always. I will say it again: **Rejoice!**"

Philippians 4:4

"Rejoice in the Lord always. I will say it again: **Rejoice!**"

Philippians 4:4

"Rejoice in the Lord always. I will say it again: **Rejoice!**"

Philippians 4:4

"Don't let anyone look down on you because you are young."

1 Timothy 4:12

"Don't let anyone look down on you because you are young."

1 Timothy 4:12

"Don't let anyone look down on you because you are young."

1 Timothy 4:12

"Don't let anyone look down on you because you are young."

1 Timothy 4:12

"BE READY TO DO WHATEVER IS GOOD."

TITUS 3:1

"BE READY TO DO WHATEVER IS GOOD."

TITUS 3:1

"BE READY TO DO WHATEVER IS GOOD."

TITUS 3:1

"BE READY TO DO WHATEVER IS GOOD."

TITUS 3:1

"*Jesus Christ* is the same yesterday and today and forever."
Hebrews 13:8

"*Jesus Christ* is the same yesterday and today and forever."
Hebrews 13:8

"*Jesus Christ* is the same yesterday and today and forever."
Hebrews 13:8

"*Jesus Christ* is the same yesterday and today and forever."
Hebrews 13:8